WRITING BIDS AND TENDERS: PROVING YOUR POINT – COLLECTING PERSUASIVE EVIDENCE FOR YOUR BID

USING A KNOWLEDGE BANK TO WIN MORE BUSINESS AND SIMPLIFY BID WRITING

Deborah E Oxberry

TABLE OF CONTENTS

INTRODUCTION

Welcome to Proving your Point – collecting persuasive evidence for your bid.

Let me start with a confession. I LOVE working on bids and tenders. In fact, I enjoy it so much that I left my job and set up my own business as a Business Development Consultant. Now I spend my days working with organisations, helping them to bid for new business. But even though it's something I really enjoy, I'm realistic too. Competitive tendering is tough. There is never enough time before the deadline, often requirements are unrealistic, the documents you have to read are endless, and the budgets are 'challenging' to say the least. As a service provider, you must complete and submit the tender alongside actually providing a service to your clients, and it can all seem a bit overwhelming. On top of that, unless you can demonstrate that your service offer is the best, then all your efforts are wasted.

I'm on a mission to make writing bids and tenders easier. But I also want to help you have more success in winning new business. This book is the first in a series that will give you some tools to both improve your bids, and make the bidding process easier.

What this book is and is not

This book is not a comprehensive guide to writing bids and tenders. There are so many aspects to that subject, that it would need a much longer book than this to cover everything. And who would have time to read it?

Instead this is a guide to one aspect of bid writing, which will help to improve your bid answers, and make the process of producing your bid document easier.

This book provides a guide to building up a knowledge bank within your organisation. This will give you easy access to evidence of your organisation's capabilities and previous experience. This can be used to reassure buyers that you can deliver what you're promising. And it will make crafting your answers easier, as you will have lots of information and data to hand to describe what you can do, and how well you can do it.

Why I wrote this book

Recently, my team was commissioned to review a bid that a client had written. It was a tender in a market the client knew well, and for a type of service that they already deliver. They had a sound service model, and some good, innovative ideas.

But there was one thing wrong – nowhere in the bid had they given any proof that they could do what they said they could.

Unfortunately, this wasn't the first time I'd had to cry "*but where is the evidence ...*?" And what followed was a very hectic and fraught 10 days as we all tried to gather information to substantiate the bid.

Why providing evidence
is important

Within competitive tendering you need to make your bid stand out from other bidders. You do this by explaining to the buyers that your service gives them substantial benefits. These benefits must meet the buyers' needs and concerns, and be unique to your offer.

But for every feature of your offer and every benefit that you outline in your bid, you must back this up with proof. Otherwise why will buyers believe that you can deliver on your offer?

Who it will help

This book is primarily aimed at organisations bidding for public sector contracts in the United Kingdom (UK). But the principles outlined in the book will be useful for anyone who is involved in producing bid documents, or managing a business development process.

The guidance in this book will be useful for organisations new to bidding, or for those who have been doing it for a while. Even if you already have a knowledge bank within your organisation, it may be helpful to revisit it using this guide. You may find extra information to add, or find a different way to use the information in a bid situation.

WRITING BIDS AND TENDERS: PROVING YOUR POINT - COLLECTING...

Assumptions I have made

This book outlines a process for providing evidence that you can deliver the features and benefits you outline in any bid that you write. My recommendation is that this process of gathering evidence should be completed outside of any tendering process, as it does take time to get it right and to gather all the information that you need.

I have assumed that you are an existing service provider, and that you will have organisational evidence to collect and store in your knowledge bank. If you are a brand-new organisation, just setting up, then use the guidance in this book to start gathering evidence as soon as you start delivering services.

A word about the language used in the book

I use the words 'bid' and 'tender' interchangeably. And I use 'offer' as shorthand for the service offer that you outline in your bid. If I'm talking about the people who receive your services, I generally use 'client' to cover client, customer, patient, carer and so on. I use the word 'buyer' to cover both commissioners and procurement staff.

What you will learn in this book

Chapters 2 to 8 in this book outline different types of evidence that you need to collect, why this evidence is important and how you would use it in your bid.

You store all your evidence in a knowledge bank, and in chapter 9 I discuss what that may look like within your organisation. I also talk about how important it is to keep the information current and updated, and how you might do this.

By the end of this book you will:

- Understand the importance of proving you can deliver your offer

- Know what types of evidence to collect

- Appreciate how to use data and other evidence within your bid

- Examine different methods of storing data

- Identify an appropriate knowledge bank for your organisation

- Outline a system of updating your knowledge bank

Next steps

This book is split into 10 chapters, and it is best if you work through the chapters in order, as each one builds on the previous ones. As a bonus for people who have purchased this book, you can download a series of checklists and templates relevant to the material covered. Details of how to do this are shown at the end in the 'next steps' section of the book.

So, let's get started.

YOUR ORGANISATION AND ITS CORPORATE BACKGROUND

Introduction

The people evaluating your bid cannot take into account any knowledge they already have about your company. That's assuming they have any knowledge of your organisation and what you do.

Sometimes the people doing the initial evaluation are not buyers, they are procurement staff, or they may not even be people at all, the initial evaluation could be done by a computer programme instead.

Often I see bids where the bidder writes as if the person evaluating has prior knowledge of their organisation, and they lose valuable points in the process. To prevent this, gather a range of information about your corporate background. This chapter covers the types of evidence that you should collect. You need to tailor this to your own organisation, but the categories listed here will give you a good starting point.

Organisational structure

It is important to have up-to-date information on your organisational structure. However, a structure chart alone just isn't enough. The information on your structure needs to provide reassurance that there is organisational oversight and assurance. Your structure needs to show where the service you are bidding to provide will 'sit' within your organisation. This should include who the service will report to and how this will ensure that the service delivered on the ground will be high quality, accountable, and have appropriate safeguards in place.

Quoting from your organisational values and mission statement

Many bidders quote their values and mission statement within their bid, but you need to do this with a purpose. If you can demonstrate how your values result in changes in your day to day practice and that these will benefit the service being procured, then that's great. But although your mission and values are very important to your organisation, they are less so to buyers, unless they lead to tangible benefits in the delivery of the service they are commissioning.

For example, if one of your organisation's values is "to achieve the best care experience for clients" then this is important ONLY if client satisfaction is one of the buyers' stated goals.

But it is no use just saying that it's one of your organisational values, you need to say how it translates into improved service on the ground. For example, you may train all your staff in customer care to a high level, involve clients in staff training and conduct regular surveys that show an increase in positive client experience.

Include this evidence in your bid and you've moved from making a statement to providing proof that you can deliver.

But remember it's only a benefit if it's something the buyer wants. If client satisfaction isn't mentioned anywhere in the specification, then it's not a priority for the buyer and won't necessarily win you extra points. And if it costs you more money to deliver then the buyer may even score you lower marks!

The trick is to link your evidence to something that the buyer *does* want. If the specification doesn't mention client satisfaction, but it does mention good joint working between staff and clients, then could you use the evidence to demonstrate how you engage and involve clients and this facilitates better joint working? And if so, can you prove it?

Added value

Before you mention things that you see as 'added value', look at them from the buyers' point of view first.

One organisation I know well was disappointed when they lost points for mentioning their national advice line – they thought this brought an extra dimension to their offer. Their advice line was based in London, and the service they were bidding for was in Leeds. Leeds buyers interpreted the inclusion of the advice line as an indication that some of their money would be used to pay "high London wages". Rather than seeing it as a benefit that provided added value, they saw it as an expensive extra that they hadn't included in the specification.

Certificates and appraisals

You also need to outline any certificates or appraisals that the organisation holds, and why these are important.

For example, say you have achieved the Investors in People Award. How does this benefit the service you're bidding for? To achieve the award, you will have had to meet certain standards. Can you give examples of these, and how achieving them will be of benefit to the buyer and meet service objectives?

If one of the standards was around good retention policies for staff (for example), this would be a benefit if continuity of care was an issue for the buyer. Because if you're good at retaining staff, then you will be able to provide clients with the same staff team on an ongoing basis.

It isn't enough just to say that you have awards, you need to say *why* they're a benefit in this service.

Memberships

It is important to have a list of any memberships that you have as an organisation, but only if you can say how the membership is of benefit. For example, you may be a member of the National Clinical Homecare Association, Skills for Care or some of the Royal Colleges. If this is part of your process for keeping up-to-date with the latest good practice and changes in legislation, then it's a benefit. Without saying what the benefits provide, memberships are pretty meaningless.

Inspection reports

Inspection reports are a good source of evidence for a bid. You can say you have good processes in place all you like, but unless someone else thinks so, the buyer will take it all with a pinch of salt.

So, use quotes from the Care Quality Commission and other inspections to prove that your processes satisfy good practice.

Pick your quotes carefully though, they need to demonstrate that you've gone above the minimum standards.

Key Personnel

You will often be asked about key personnel within your organisation. This is to demonstrate that you have good leadership, from people with relevant experience and who hold a certain level of expertise. It is important to have up-to-date resumes for senior personnel, but these need to include more than just a list of qualifications. Relate their qualifications and experience to the service that you're bidding for. It is important to keep up-to-date with awards and commendations that staff have obtained so that you can cite them when they are relevant. Also to know the size and scope of the services that staff have been responsible for, and how they will use the experience and skills that they have to improve this service.

Expert staff can be a key discriminator if you present them in the right way.

Organisational history
and overview

As I mentioned before, evaluators can only evaluate what is in the bid, so do not assume they know anything about your company. It is quite easy to do this accidentally. I have often reviewed bids where the bidders talk about a particular service by its name, such as "Healthy Living, Anytown" without going on to explain anything about it. This is quite annoying if you're reading a bid, as you find yourself thinking "Am I supposed to know what that is?"

It's important to have a concise history and overview of your company that you can modify for each bid. This includes an organisational history, your existing services, locations, types of services, geographical spread and the demographic details of the clients that you provide services for.

You want the evaluator to read this and get a picture of the size and scope of your organisation, and also how your experience is relevant to the service that you're bidding for.

It is also a good idea to have basic facts about your organisation easily accessible in one place, e.g. company registration number, charity number, VAT number, and other standard information that you will have to quote for prequalification.

Benchmarking

If you can benchmark your service delivery against national or regional standards, then this adds another dimension to the statistics you can quote about your performance.

For example, if you say that you respond to referrals
within 10 days 74% of the time, then I wouldn't know if
this was good or not. Tell me that the national average
is 54% and I can see immediately that you're providing a
good service. Analyse your data regularly, and keep an up-
to-date record of your performance.

Policies and Processes

Easy access to policies and processes is very important, especially for pre-qualification or one stage bidding processes, as you'll usually be asked to provide a range of your policies.

You need a process to keep your policies current, and to make sure they reflect changes in best practice, legislative changes, and organisational changes. They also need to be dated, and regularly updated. I have worked with good companies who have been disqualified because their policies have been out-of-date, or not appropriately authorised. Do not make that mistake.

I have also worked with companies where they have purchased template policies, then, apart from adding their company name, haven't got around to finalising them. For example, I recently worked with a company that had a business continuity policy, but they hadn't completed the 'business risks' table. The policy had to be submitted with the bid, so in effect they did not have an effective process in place to respond to business continuity risks.

There are some policies that you will nearly always have to produce. They include health and safety, data protection, clinical governance, complaints, safeguarding and equal opportunities. It is important that these policies are complete and up-to-date, but also that they're backed up with organisational processes and systems. Your health and safety policy should link to a robust system of risk assessments, and you should be able to name the 're- sponsible person' for health and safety advice, and state their credentials. You should know your registration number with the Information Commissioner's office, details of your Caldicott Guardian, details of any data breaches that you've had, and how you resolved them and learned from them.

You should be able to describe how your clinical governance policy works in practice, how many complaints you've had, and whether they are increasing and decreasing, and any trends. Also collect figures on any safeguarding complaints against you, and how you resolved these.

Each policy needs to be cross-referenced with organisational systems, personnel, reporting arrangements, and have data to back up how effective your policy is. You should also be able to describe how you train or inform staff about their obligations under the policy, and how you ensure they understand what is expected of them, and how you refresh their knowledge. This sounds like a lot, but it all provides reassurance that your policies are not just meaningless pieces of paper.

Additional information

Another couple of areas that are increasingly asked about in bids are Corporate Social Responsibility (CSR) and Sustainability. Gather some narrative and facts and figures to explain your commitment to both of these areas.

For example, what steps are you taking to reduce your carbon footprint? What impact has this had? How many of your staff live locally to where they work? By showing that the majority of the staff live locally, you can demonstrate that you are reducing mileage costs and the impact on the environment. You are also boosting the local economy by providing employment for local people, who will go on to spend their wages in local businesses. Do you support local charities? If so, how, and how has this helped the local community?

Corporate background – summary

Organisational information is important to demonstrate that your business systems are robust and updated regularly, either because of legislative changes or lessons learned. But it's not enough to say that you have systems in place, you must be able to back these up with evidence, and also place them in context to show that you can offer more than your competitors.

EVIDENCE ABOUT YOUR PAST PERFORMANCE

In the introduction I explained it is important to provide evidence in bids, as by providing proof you reassure buyers that you can deliver on your bid offer.

I suggested that building up a knowledge bank of evidence should be done outside of the tender process, as it does take time to get it right. I also stressed the importance of having a system in place to keep the information in your knowledge bank up-to-date.

In the previous chapter I started to look at the types of evidence that you should gather and store, starting with information about your corporate background. In this chapter I will continue to discuss the types of evidence that you should collect and store in your knowledge bank, concentrating on evidence related to past performance.

Why your past performance is important

Awarding a contract is always a huge risk for a buyer. They need reassurance that you will deliver what is expected, within stated timescales, and to the quality that they expect. Unless buyers invent time travel or a crystal ball so they can look ahead and see how you'll deliver the service, they have to find this reassurance through the tendering process. One of the best ways that you can convince them that you are the right organisation to deliver the contract is to demonstrate relevant past performance.

You should collect and regularly update data relating to your existing and past contracts, and your performance in running those services.

What information should you collect?

The information you need to collect includes:

- A list of the services you deliver

- Size of your current services

- Contract values

- Numbers of clients

- Numbers and grades of staff

- Geographical coverage

- Population size

- Population demographics

This information can be used to show where you have previous experience in service delivery, and to put this in some sort of context. You can demonstrate that you have experience of running services of a similar size, in a similar location, or of employing the range of staff necessary to deliver the service you're bidding for. This is all useful to demonstrate your organisational capacity and capabilities.

Analysing data

You also need to regularly collect data about your performance. Obviously you should be doing this anyway to meet your contract reporting requirements. But you may need to collect more information than you currently do and record this for use in bids. Include details of your performance against key performance indicators (KPIs), include details of any incentives that you've earned, and any cost savings that you've made.

It is not enough to gather the data; you need to analyse it. Obviously, showing that you can meet or exceed performance expectations is a good start, but you can gain a lot more from an analysis of service data.

Imagine you provide services mainly to adults, but you would like to bid for a contract to deliver services for older people. If you analyse the demographics of your existing services, you may find that many of your existing clients are over 60 years of age. This gives you evidence that you can gain good outcomes for this client group, and you can include this within your tender.

Maximising good outcomes

If you have a particularly good outcome in one area, analyse how you have achieved it. This can sometimes take a bit of thought, but it's worth doing.

For example, I worked with some clients in a clinical service who had a 100% success rate in preventing infections. When I asked 'how do you achieve that', they initially weren't able to tell me. Was it just a fluke? No, when I questioned them closely, I discovered that they actually had lots of good systems in place to avoid infection. They were so used to doing it, that they didn't even think about it anymore. But by describing exactly what they would do to avoid infection, and then saying they know this works as they had a 100% non-infection rate, the company scored top marks for that part of the bid.

Dealing with poor results

If you've had poor results in the past, use these to your advantage – assuming you've done something to correct them of course!

Describe how you closely analyse your service performance, how you spotted something wasn't working, and how you did a root cause analysis to find out why. Explain the measures you took to bring performance back on track and the lessons you learned from this to ensure it doesn't happen again.

By being upfront you provide reassurance to the buyers that you have systems in place to spot if the service isn't working, and that you'll do something about it quickly. If you can also say how you worked with buyers in a positive and open way to resolve performance issues, then this will provide even more reassurance.

Past Performance – summary

Have a system in place to share performance data from services with your business development team. Where you have particularly good data, analyse what it is you do that makes your performance so good. And use poor performance positively to demonstrate that you work proactively with buyers to resolve anything that goes wrong, as quickly as possible. This will help to reassure buyers that they can trust you to deliver a good service.

AUDIT DATA

Introduction

In the last chapter, I looked at evidence about your past performance. Linked to that, it is important that you have easy access to audit data, and that you interpret this data so that it can be used to back up what you're saying in a bid.

You will probably carry out a range of audits in your organisation. You should have regular schedules where you audit data, clinical records, service quality, staff development and the outcomes that clients have achieved. Each organisation will have a range of different audits, depending on the types of services that you provide.

Describing your audit process

You need a description of how you carry out your audits. This should include how often they are done, who does them, what tools and processes you use, who is responsible in the organisation for ensuring audits happen, and how your senior team monitors and acts on audit information.

You should also have details of external and independent audits carried out, as these provide particularly good evidence for the quality and efficiency of your services.

Analysing audit data

It is not enough to have an audit system in place, you need to analyse the data you get from your audit processes.

For example, I worked with a client lately who was very proud of the fact that they had increased their patient numbers substantially since they took over a particular clinical service 3 years ago. But I was puzzled - what did that actually mean? Did it mean that they don't discharge patients when they should? Or that their patients become overly dependent on their services? In either case, that's not something you want to highlight.

Alternatively, it could mean that their services are so easily accessible and welcoming that people choose to engage with them rather than other providers. Perhaps they're proactive at reaching 'hard to reach' groups and that's how they've boosted patient numbers? Or they're really good at health promotion, and so people come in for screening and wellbeing services? If this is the case, then you have a really good story to tell. Data without analysis and explanation doesn't provide that positive story.

After you have analysed what the figures mean, and what they demonstrate about your practice, you should say how this relates to the specification for the service you're bidding for. If there is a big emphasis in the specification on self-management and reducing demand on services, then you need to use your data about increasing patient numbers very carefully! On the other hand, if buyers are concerned about certain parts of the population not accessing services, and you can demonstrate that you reach these groups, this is going to result in extra marks for your bid.

Maximising good results
and innovations

Where your audits do show really good results, then make sure you can explain how you've achieved these. You want to demonstrate that this was a planned approach, in response to an issue or problem. It is not so much of an achievement if it happened accidentally!

If you have anything innovative that you've introduced, such as the use of assistive technology, or effective staff rostering, then make sure you mention how these have contributed to positive outcomes.

I worked with a Home Care provider who introduced a new rota system that significantly reduced travel time for their workers. This resulted in 98% of all care calls starting within 10 minutes of their allocated time. You can imagine, if you're old, alone, and with limited mobility, if you're expecting a care worker at 8am to help you get up and dressed, you're pretty fed up if they don't turn up until 9am. Clients had expressed their dissatisfaction to buyers about poor timekeeping. Buyers, in turn, asked a question in a subsequent bid about how providers could address this. My client scored higher marks because they could provide evidence that they had already identified and addressed this issue, and were consistently reaching people on time.

Describing your achievements

If you have any specific achievements, then make sure you have full details of these. This could include awards that you've won, or perhaps other services have adopted your processes because they demonstrate best practice in your field. Tenders these days nearly always ask for innovation, and if you can describe innovative approaches and how these have led to auditable service improvements, you will have a positive story to tell.

Sharing audit data

Put systems in place to share your audit data with the team producing your bid response. Analyse the data so that you can demonstrate what you've done to achieve good results, and how this relates to the service that is being tendered.

Audit data – summary

Audit data can provide good evidence to demonstrate your processes are effective. You need to provide assurance that your systems are robust and logical, and that you are comfortable with analysing and using data positively.

It is important that you have easy access to up-to-date data, so incorporate a process of updating your knowledge bank regularly.

QUALITY PROCESSES

Introduction

In chapters 3 and 4 I looked at gathering data about your service performance. This chapter shifts focus a bit, to look instead at your organisational processes, and your quality processes in particular.

You will usually find at least one question in every tender questionnaire about quality processes. Often there is a whole section. In my experience organisations often answer these questions badly. This is mainly because they talk about their processes, but fail to explain how these lead to good quality service delivery, and how they would be applied in the service they are tendering for.

So as you gather your evidence, think about how you can explain your quality processes in a way that creates a direct link between what you do, and how this assures a good level of service quality.

Describing your quality processes

All organisations should have a documented quality process. If this is externally verified and audited, then this is even better. Although I do come across a number of organisations who have achieved a quality mark, such as ISO 9001, but it only covers a small part of their organisation, for example their financial systems. This often leads to the organisation becoming complacent about quality processes in other areas. If they are then asked to describe how they will ensure the quality of their service delivery, they really begin to struggle.

A quality management process is a set of procedures that you follow to ensure that your service is 'fit for purpose'. You will set targets (such as Key Performance Indicators) with your buyer, and you may also want to set your own internal targets. You then implement a quality assurance and quality control process to measure and report the actual quality of the service you deliver. Part of the process is to identify any quality issues and resolve them as soon as possible.

In order to outline your processes in a bid, you need to be able to describe:

- How you identify and set targets

- How you measure and report on the quality of your service

- Who does this, how they do it and when

- Who reviews the outcomes, and decides to take action where needed

- How identified actions are monitored for implementation

- Your process for quality improvement on a continuous basis

- You also need to cover your reporting procedures

Proving that your quality system works

To evidence that the system works, give examples of how the processes you have in place have directly led to improved quality in service delivery. Statistics alone do not do this; you need to back it up with explanations.

As your quality process covers all parts of your organisation, the examples you give should relate to the particular part of the bid that you're answering. For example, if you're in the Human Resources section, talk about how you ensure the quality of your staff team. If the question is about your quality process itself, then you can pick a number of examples that most effectively demonstrate your system in use.

Quality Processes - Summary

Within bids you should be able to describe a documented quality assurance process, preferably externally accredited and audited.

The process will describe how you set targets, how you measure progress against those targets and how you report on progress. Your description needs to include who does what, how they do it and how often. You also need to explain who reviews the outcomes, and decides to take action where it is needed, and how these actions are monitored. You should also describe your continuous improvement process.

Statistics alone do not tell the full story; you need to also describe how the systems you have in place have directly led to improved quality in service delivery.

INFORMATION RELATED TO CLIENTS (AND CARERS)

Introduction

Bidding for services in a health and social care context is slightly unusual, in that during the tendering process, the buyers are your 'customers' as they are buying your products or services. But the end users of your services are the patients/clients/service users who will receive what you are offering, along with their families and carers. In this book I use the term 'client' as shorthand for patients, clients, families and carers.

I have seen organisations concentrate solely on describing organisational systems and processes, where clients seem to be missed out altogether. I have also seen other bids where the focus is totally on the client, with no reassurance about organisational capability or governance. It is important to get the balance right, and to explain how your systems achieve the desired outcomes for individuals.

Client (and carer) data needs to relate to two main areas:

- Client involvement and engagement

- Client experience

Client involvement and engagement

With an increasing focus on person-centred services, it is important that you have good systems in place to involve clients in the development and ongoing running of your services. This includes everything from decisions about their own care, to being involved in monitoring your services and ensuring that there is a continuous improvement plan in place.

Very often I find that organisations will hear the latest buzz word about client involvement and decide to use that in their bids. A recent example is 'coproduction'. Many clients will tell me they 'coproduce' their services with clients. But they have no evidence or even feasible explanation of how they do this. Coproduction is an approach that involves changes to your culture, structure and practice, and which needs to be reviewed regularly. It is not enough to say that you do it, you have to explain how it's been embedded into your organisational culture and practice.

Whatever systems you use to involve clients, make sure you capture the outcomes. For example, a client told me that they had involved young people in redesigning a website for a young person's service, to make it more age-appropriate. What they couldn't actually tell me was whether this resulted in more young people accessing the website, downloading resources and accessing their service - so it wasn't a very strong example to use. But it could have been if they'd had the data to back it up. Involvement has to be meaningful and it has to produce outcomes.

Incidentally, I very rarely come across organisations that

ask clients how they feel about the involvement they've had, and whether it works for them. This seems to be a big gap – how do you know that clients feel involved and engaged unless you ask them?

Client experience

There is a lot of material that you can collect relating to client experience. The first, and arguably most important, is patient outcome data. All services now are outcome-focussed, and so you need to have good ways of identifying the outcomes that people want to achieve, and to measure these. This seems obvious, but so many clients tell me that they 'review goals regularly', but they cannot give me statistics on how many goals have been achieved, or even how many clients have achieved *any* goals. You need to find a way to measure and report on this.

If possible, split outcome data down further and analyse it. Do you get particularly good outcomes with certain demographic groups, for example? If so, why? Are there other groups that aren't achieving outcomes? What can you do about this? Showing that you have analysed and acted on outcome data is probably something that your competitors won't be able to offer, and is a sign of a very effectively run service.

Other useful data includes safeguarding issues and how they were resolved. And complaints, compliments and testimonials.

Service user surveys can provide useful statistics, plus usable quotes if there is a 'free text' section. Surveys should be recent and have a high return rate to be meaningful.

Case studies can really bring a bid to life if they are used carefully. Unfortunately, I have seen them used very badly. The main problem is where the case study does not adequately illustrate the point you're trying to make, or even worse, negates it. For example, in a bid where the emphasis was on self-reliance, there was a case study that explained how a client's life had changed, but everything he'd achieved involved support workers doing things for him – not a good example of fostering self-reliance!

If the case study does not clearly illustrate the point that you're making in that section of the bid, then it's probably the wrong case study to use.

Other problems with case studies is that they can often give too much irrelevant detail, whilst not explaining what the service did to help. It is a good idea to have a template for case studies, so that they can be collected routinely, in a similar format. Basically you need; some background information, what the problem was. What the service did to help resolve the problem, and what the (positive) outcome was for the client. Using this format, you can show a lot in a very few words.

Accessibility

With all client involvement and experience opportunities, you should demonstrate how they are accessible to everyone. How do you get the views of people with reduced mental capacity? What about people who have communication problems? Do you reach out to 'hard to reach' groups?

Client Information - Summary

Service user and carer data is vital to provide evidence for your capabilities in service delivery. Collect evidence relating to client involvement and engagement, and client experience, and make sure you collect this on an ongoing basis.

As well as the checklist for this chapter, there is an extra file for you to download. This is a template for you to collect case studies in a consistent format. Used well, case studies can demonstrate how effective your services are in obtaining outcomes, and do so using only a few words. This is particularly useful when you have a tight word count!

STAFF DETAILS

Introduction

In the last chapter, I looked at the sorts of information you should gather relating to clients. In this chapter I look at another important group of people – your staff team.

Staff are one of the most vital components in good service delivery, so you need to demonstrate that you can attract and retain good staff, and support them to deliver high-quality services. There are often whole sections in a bid on staffing, simply because it is so important. Having good quality information available will help you to craft compelling answers and prove you have the organisational capability to provide an effective staff team. Policies and processes are important, but so is data to demonstrate that your processes deliver what they are supposed to.

Proving that your policies and processes work – gathering data

Data that it would be useful to have to hand includes:

- The number of staff that you employ in different grades

- Details of the registrations, certifications, qualifications, and any clearances that staff already hold

- CVs/resumes of key personnel

- Training records and any awards that staff have achieved

- Retention rates, both company-wide and service-specific

You can use this data to demonstrate that the processes you have in place work, and to answer points in the bid. For example, continuity of care leads to safer services and is preferred by clients. This often makes it a priority for buyers. If you can demonstrate that you have good retention processes in place, and prove this by having statistics on your staff retention rates, then this provides a robust answer, with evidence to back it up.

You should also compare this with regional or national averages in your sector to put the statistics in context. Average figures should be available from professional associations, such as 'Skills for Care' www.skillsforcare.org.uk

Recruitment processes and statistics

Record full details of your recruitment processes, including the type of interview questions that you ask, what training your recruiters undertake, and pre-employment checks that you carry out. You should also document how these processes ensure that you have safe, competent staff in place, rather than leaving the buyer to assume that they do. So explain why you carry out pre-employment checks (for example), and how this benefits buyers.

Useful statistics relating to recruitment include the number of vacancies that you have, the average time you take to fill different positions, which recruitment methods you use, the number of recruiters you have and your sources of recruitment.

By having this information to hand, you can describe, in a convincing way, that you will be able to recruit an appropriate team for any new service you are commissioned to provide.

Coping with fluctuating demands

Many services that you will be bidding for have fluctuating demands. Commissioners no longer want to pay for staff sitting around doing nothing, so think about how you can build flexibilities within your workforce to cope with peaks and troughs in demand.

You also need to think about contingencies if key staff leave, or you have sickness or other absence. It is not enough to just describe the plans that you have, you need to explain why you know that these plans will work. At all costs avoid saying "it's never happened, so we're not worried." You wouldn't do that? Good, you'd be surprised by the number of people who do!

Service mobilisation

Commissioners will want reassurance that you will be able to mobilise the service on time. It is very rare that there isn't a question on service mobilisation or transition within a bid.

You need to designate someone to lead the mobilisation, preferably someone with similar experience, which should be documented. Don't just say they're experienced, you need to say how many times they have mobilised a service, the size of the service they have set up (i.e. number of staff and clients) and how it is similar to the service you're bidding for.

You also need to talk about the method you will use to manage the mobilisation, and describe the full mobilisation team and the specific expertise that they bring. If you use a recognised project management approach, that's great, explain what it is, how your team is qualified to use it, and what the process will look like.

If you're not using a specific project management methodology, explain how often the team will meet, what the different roles will be, how you will measure progress, and what action you will take if the mobilisation isn't progressing as it should. You should include details of how you will alert buyers to any problems, and your risk management plan.

Transferring staff under TUPE

Quite often, if the service you're bidding for already exists, then you will have to describe how you will transfer staff under the Transfer of Undertakings (Protection of Employment) Regulations (TUPE). You should describe your previous experience of doing this, plus explain who will provide professional support to ensure that you follow due process. If you can evidence that staff that you have previously transferred have stayed with your organisation, then this demonstrates that you have carried out an effective transfer and integrated the staff into your organisation successfully.

A good plan, plus confirmation that you've achieved mobilisation in similar services, will help to reassure buyers about your ability to set up the service and 'go live' on time.

Staff development

Tenders will often ask about how you develop your staff, and so you will need to describe your supervision and appraisal processes, and the training that you can provide. Details of your training budget demonstrates that you have a commitment to staff development, but be careful that you're only training your staff in a way that will improve service delivery. Buyers do not want to pay for unnecessary qualifications for staff.

You need to ensure that all professional staff are able to satisfy the Continuing Professional Development or CPD requirements of their registrations, and that all staff have the opportunity to complete qualifications relevant to their post.

Induction training for all staff is important, along with mandatory and refresher training. Additional personal development should be described in terms of the benefits it can bring to the service. For example, say you run a home care service. If you can offer your staff training in delegated nursing tasks, this will free up valuable District Nursing time, and cost less to the local health economy. Therefore, this is a sensible development for the service and for your staff.

Consulting and involving staff

The person-centred approach to service delivery also applies to staff, so you should have systems in place to consult with staff and involve them in service development and delivery. Again you should be able to describe these processes and give examples of what has been achieved through their application.

An example of this that I've come across recently was a client who introduced a loan car for home care staff. This was available free of charge if a staff member's own vehicle was in for repair. The loan car was introduced after a consultation session with staff about how to reduce last minute absences. Following its introduction, last minute absence was reduced by 50% within the next 3 months. A great example of listening to staff, finding out what was causing problems, and coming up with a solution that had a positive impact.

Happy staff give a better service, so staff satisfaction surveys, carried out regularly, can provide evidence that staff are happy with the support and opportunities that you offer, and with their work environment.

Staff details - Summary

The fact that there are so many questions about staffing in tenders shows how important this is to buyers. With a good description of your processes, supported by relevant data, you can maximise your scores in this area.

Prove that your policies and processes work by backing them up with data to show how effective they are. Demonstrate your experience in establishing and training staff teams to meet service demands. Show how you can build flexibilities into your staffing model to cope with peaks and troughs in demand, and that you listen to your staff and act on what they tell you.

In this way, you will demonstrate that you will be able to attract and retain an appropriate staff team to provide a high quality service.

PARTNERSHIP WORKING AND STAKEHOLDER ENGAGEMENT

Introduction

Tender questions about joint working and stakeholder engagement are often the most difficult to answer clearly. Many answers that I've seen tend to be abstract, because, unless you're the current provider, you probably haven't engaged these stakeholders successfully already. If you have plenty advanced notice of the bid coming out, you can start some stakeholder engagement (whilst being aware of competition rules), but if this is not possible, you need to have a good plan for stakeholder engagement. This should outline who you will engage with, how you'll engage with them, the purpose of that engagement, who will do it (this should be someone fairly senior), and how you will monitor and measure success. You should describe engagement during mobilisation and on an ongoing basis, once you start delivering the service.

Using examples effectively

To back up your plan, you should gather examples of good joint working from existing services. These should describe what you did, and what the outcome was. For example, did joint working provide efficiencies or lead to improved outcomes for clients?

Where can joint working help?

Think about the client pathway and where there may be weak points that joint working can address.

One of my clients delivered a service where many of the people referred to it had problems, but did not meet the criteria for the service. These people ended up being 'bounced' back and forward between the service and their General Practitioner (GP), without getting any help at all. Through developing a partnership with a local voluntary sector organisation, they were able to refer people to an alternative source of help. This reduced the workload of both GPs and the service and meant that people were able to get the help they needed.

Partnership Working and Stake-holder Engagement - Summary

Try to avoid abstract answers about joint working and stakeholder engagement, make a list of the stakeholders you will engage with, and who you will need to work with in order to provide a comprehensive service and achieve service outcomes. If you have time, start to implement your plan before you submit the tender.

You should be able to describe a credible plan, and back this up with examples from other services that demonstrate you know how to engage other organisations and work in partnership. Examples should always explain the benefits or improved outcomes achieved through joint working.

This is the last chapter that looks at gathering evidence, next I'll move onto developing your knowledge bank and keeping the information updated. In this book I have covered the most common types of evidence that you need for the majority of bids. Depending on your organisation and the services you deliver, there may be other types of evidence that you need to collect. It will be useful to look at some of your past tenders and see if you can identify any other types of information that you need to store in your knowledge bank.

STORING EVIDENCE AND KEEPING IT UPDATED

Introduction

Producing a tender document is always time-limited and stressful. Gathering the information I have described will help you to back up your service solution with evidence of your capability to provide the service. But for this information to be useful, it needs to be accessible, and that means having a good system of storage and a method of updating the information. You need to develop some form of knowledge bank.

Developing the knowledge bank needs to be someone's job, otherwise it won't be a priority and it won't happen. If you can appoint someone as coordinator, and then allocate specific updating tasks to other people, then that will usually be sufficient. It isn't a full-time job but you do need to allocate some time to establishing it in the first place.

Establishing your knowledge bank

I have seen lots of different storage methods for knowledge banks, and these vary depending on the complexity and size of the organisation. One small organisation simply had a ring binder with different sections. This was useful as when new information came in, such as the results of the patient survey, they could be easily added to the folder. Other organisations have used a shared 'drive' or file on the computer, or other sharing software packages such as One Note, Dropbox or SharePoint.

Most organisations use the company intranet to store the information, so that it's easily accessible to everyone.

Whatever storage method you use, you should have an introductory page, giving an overview of the different sections within the knowledge bank, and what's contained within each section. The areas outlined in previous chapters would be a good starting point, that is:

- Corporate background

- Past performance

- Audit data

- Quality processes

- Information related to clients

- Staff details

- Partnership working and stakeholder engagement

Within each section, you should then have different subsections, containing the information that you collect, and it helps if this is in a standard format, so it's easy to extract the information that you need. You can use the downloaded checklists to gather the information I have

suggested and add other information relevant to your particular organisation and service types.

Keeping your knowledge bank updated

Identify a system for updating each section of your knowledge bank. This doesn't need to be complicated. Some sections, particularly those that describe your processes, just need to be refreshed annually, or if your processes change.

When I have worked with companies to set up a knowledge bank, I have devised a simple spreadsheet, just indicating when updating needs to take place. These dates can then be entered into the appropriate person's diary as a task or alert.

Other information needs to be updated more regularly, such as audit data. The trick is to incorporate updating your knowledge bank into your audit cycle, so that as audit results are published, they are automatically sent to the person responsible for coordinating the knowledge bank. Develop a similar system for staff and client surveys, complaints monitoring, and recording safeguarding issues. It is good practice for your senior team to monitor all of this data anyway, so as the senior team receives a report, there should also be a system to report to the knowledge bank coordinator.

In this way, you always have up-to-date information to hand, whenever you have a tender on the go. Setting up the initial knowledge bank does take some time, but think of it as an investment as it saves time further down the line. A systematic approach to updating is needed to ensure the initial investment yields the desired results.

Software

There are a range of software options that you can buy, designed specifically to store evidence for bids.

If you search 'bid management software' in your search engine, a list will come up. I have experienced some of these software packages, and they vary in quality and ease of use. Most companies are willing to give you a free demonstration of the software, and you will need to decide if the cost is justified depending on the number of bids that you do each year. You may also need to consider if these systems will work with your existing technology.

Professional support to set up
a bespoke knowledge bank

Another option you may like to consider is bringing in a professional business development support company to help you establish a knowledge bank, as a one-off project. This means that the knowledge bank is tailored exactly to your company and how you will use it. This is a useful option if you do not have the resources within your company to set up your knowledge bank. You must be prepared to work closely with the consultants you bring in, so that you end up with something that exactly meets your needs.

Storing and updating your information - Summary

Allocate time and resources to establishing a knowledge bank, and make it part of someone's job, or it just won't happen. The time spent initially will be regained later on, as you will have easy access to information when you are writing bids, making the whole process easier and less stressful. Access to good proof of your organisational capabilities will also improve the quality of the bids you submit.

Your knowledge bank storage system should reflect the needs of your organisation and take into account who gets involved in writing bids, and where they are located. If all of your bid team are in one office, then paper files may well do the job. If the team is dispersed, then find an electronic method of sharing files.

Whatever method you use, your storage systems needs to be logical and well indexed so that people can find the information they need easily and quickly.

Having a good updating system is vital. Look at how often the information changes and schedule updates as appropriate. Wherever possible incorporate updating your knowledge bank into your existing processes, as it is much more likely to get done, and it will be much more efficient.

Task people with updating information relating to their particular area of responsibility within your organisation. There should also be an overall coordinator who will check on a regular basis that updating is happening and that out-of-date information has been removed.

With a little bit of planning maintaining a knowledge bank

does not need to be time-consuming.

There are bespoke software solutions that help you to establish a knowledge bank, or a business development company will establish a bespoke solution as a one-off project. If you opt for either of these options you must allow time to work with either the software company, or the consultants, to set up the initial information. And of course, you will still need to establish an updating method.

Whatever route you choose, don't be daunted by the task. Not only does establishing a knowledge bank help you in future tenders, it also helps you to think through why you do things in a certain way, and what you do with information that you gather in your organisation. Some companies find that the process helps them to streamline and improve their systems, which is an unexpected bonus that helps the company outside of the tender process.

Summary

Congratulations, we've reached the final chapter of the book. I hope you're ready to get started on establishing your knowledge bank, the first step to improving your bids. Remember that time invested now will reduce stress later on, when you are working through a bid process.

In this chapter I will recap on what we have covered so far, and revisit the learning objectives.

REVISITING THE LEARNING OBJECTIVES

In chapter one I explored why it is important to provide proof that you can deliver on the offer you outline in your bid. This provides reassurance to buyers that they can trust you to deliver the service well, and proves that you have transferable and verifiable experience. Providing proof that you can deliver on what you say makes your bid stand out from competitors and gives you an advantage in the bidding process.

In chapters 2 through to 8, I looked at the types of evidence to collect. This includes information relating to past and current performance, descriptions of your processes and how these directly lead to the provision of a good quality service. I provided access to checklists to help you to gather relevant information within your own organisation.

It is not enough to just gather data and other evidence, you have to use this appropriately within your bid, to support the point that you are trying to make. The general rule is to try and prove every point. If you say you can deliver outcome-focussed services, say how many of your current clients have set and achieved outcomes, and explain how this happens within your organisation. If you offer to mobilise the service on time, explain your staff recruitment processes and give examples from other services that you have mobilised on time, of a similar size and in a similar area. Reassure the buyer at every point, demonstrating that you're the best company to deliver the service that they are tendering.

In chapter 9 I outlined some different ways of storing the information you gather for your knowledge bank. This needs to fit your organisation's needs and be accessible to people who both use it and update it.

How much you invest in establishing a knowledge bank depends on the size and complexity of your organisation and how many bids you submit each year. Professional help is available, but even an in-house solution has a cost in terms of use of internal resources. Try to balance the resources needed to establish the knowledge bank against the savings in time preparing tenders, and the increased likelihood of winning new business. Some organisations also find additional benefits, as establishing the knowledge bank is a good way to revisit and streamline existing processes.

If you spend time establishing a knowledge bank, then this is wasted unless you also have a system of regular updating. Build this into existing systems and allocate a coordinator to check it's happening, and this needn't be too much of a chore. Carrying out small updates regularly is much more effective than a huge update less frequently. It also means that the latest information is available when you need it for a bid.

LEARNING FROM BIDS

After each bid process you should ask for feedback from buyers, whether you win or lose. Ask them which proof points were most compelling, and gather more of this type of evidence within your knowledge bank.

FINAL NOTE

By building up a knowledge bank of evidence, you can pepper your bid with proof points that assure evaluators that the features and benefits that you claim within your bid are real, verifiable and achievable. This reduces your risk as a provider, and makes your bid more interesting and compelling.

NEXT STEPS

Download the checklists and other resources

Please go to https://deborahoxberry.com/bonus-material and download the file called 'Bonus materials'.

PLEASE PROVIDE FEEDBACK

If you enjoyed this book, or even just found it useful, please leave a review at Amazon. This doesn't need to be long, a line or two would do. It makes a difference to others who may benefit from the book. And of course, it means a lot to me. Thank you!

You can jump right to the page by clicking below:

US

UK

FURTHER INFORMATION

I have provided a list of Resources on the next page which relate to things I've mentioned in this book, and that you may find useful.

However, your first task is to establish your knowledge bank, and implement your system of updating. Good luck and here's to happy and successful bidding!

RESOURCES

This is a list of terms that I've used within the book with definitions, links or further information, as appropriate.

Investors in People

Investors in People (IiP) is a UK nationally recognised framework that helps organisations to improve their performance and realise their objectives through the effective management and development of their staff teams.

http://www.investorsinpeople.com

National Home Care Association

United Kingdom Homecare Association Ltd (UKHCA) is the professional association of home care providers from the independent, voluntary, not-for-profit and statutory sectors. UKHCA helps organisations that provide social care to people in their own homes deliver high standards of care and provides representation with national and regional policy-makers and regulators.

http://www.ukhca.co.uk

Skills for Care

Skills for Care is the employer-led workforce development body for adult social care in England. They offer workforce led support and practical resources to help raise quality and standards across the whole sector.

http://www.skillsforcare.org.uk

Royal Colleges

There are several Royal Colleges relevant to health and social care in the UK, such as the Royal College of Nursing, which is the world's largest nursing union and professional body.

http://www.rcn.org.uk

Care Quality Commission

The Care Quality Commission (CQC) is the independent regulator of health and social care in England.

http://www.cqc.org.uk

Company Registration Number

A company registration number (CRN) is a unique eight-character reference assigned to a company upon its incorporation. Companies House provides this identifying number and it is printed on your company's certificate of incorporation.

https://www.gov.uk/government/organisations/companies-house

Charity Number

When a charity has income over £5,000 per year, and is based in England or Wales, they must register with the Charity Commission, who registers and regulates charities. The commission issues charities with a unique registration number.

https://www.gov.uk/government/organisations/charity-commission

VAT Number

A value added tax identification number of VAT identification number is an identifier used for value added tax purposes. VAT registration numbers are issued by HMRC (Her

Majesty's Revenue and Customs)

https://www.gov.uk/government/organisations/hm-revenue-customs

Health and Safety Responsible Person
The Management of Health and Safety at Work Regulations 1999 states that you must get help from a competent person to enable you to meet the requirements of health and safety law. A competent person is someone who has sufficient training and experience or knowledge and other qualities that allow them to assist you properly.

http://www.hse.gov.uk

Information Commissioner's Office
The Information Commissioner's Officer (ICO) is responsible for the enforcement of the Data Protection Act 1998, and also responsible for Freedom of Information. They keep a register of data controllers, including organisations that process personal data.

http://www.ico.org.uk

Caldicott Guardian
A Caldicott Guardian is a senior person responsible for protecting the confidentiality of patient and service-user information and enabling appropriate information-sharing. Each National Health Service (NHS) and Social Care organisation is required to have a Caldicott Guardian.

https://www.gov.uk/government/groups/uk-caldicott-guardian-council

Key Performance Indicators (KPIs)
A KPI is a measurable value that demonstrates how effectively a company is achieving key business objectives

Root Cause Analysis

Root Cause Analysis is a method of problem-solving used for identifying the root causes of faults or problems.

ISO 9001

ISO 9001 is a global benchmark for quality management and sets the requirements of a quality management system.

http://www.iso.org

Coproduction

This is one definition of coproduction, "a way of working whereby citizens and decision-makers, or people who use services, family carers and service providers work together to create a decision or service which works for them all. The approach is value-driven and built on the principle that those who use a service are best placed to help design it."

For further information see the Social Care Institute for Excellence

http://www.scie.org.uk

TUPE

TUPE refers to the "Transfer of Undertakings (Protection of Employment) Regulations 2006 and subsequent amendments. The TUPE rules apply to organisations of all sizes and protect employees' rights when the organisation or service they work for transfers to a new employer.

http://www.acas.org.uk

Continuing Professional Development (CPD)

CPD is the process of tracking and documenting the skills, knowledge and experience that employees gain both formally and informally as they work, beyond any initial training. It is a record of what staff experience, learn and then apply. Many professional bodies have ongoing CPD requirements as a condition of continued registration.

Delegated Nursing Tasks

Tasks normally carried out by Registered Nurses can be delegated to other staff, such as a Health Care Assistant, as long as they have been trained to carry out the tasks, they are competent to do so, and are adequately supervised and supported. Search for 'accountability and delegation' for further information.

http://www.rcn.org.uk

District Nurses

District Nurses are senior nurses in the UK's National Health Service who manage care within the community, leading teams of community nurses and support workers, as well as visiting house-bound patients to provide advice and care.

General Practitioners (GPs)

GPs are medical doctors who look after the health of people in their local community and deal with a whole range of health problems. They also provide health education, screening, vaccinations and carry out simple surgical procedures. They usually work with a team including nurses, health visitors, midwives and a range of other health professionals such as physiotherapists and occupational therapists.

http://www.rcgp.org.uk

One Note

Microsoft OneNote is a computer program for free-form information-gathering and multi-user collaboration.

http://www.onenote.com

DropBox

Dropbox is a file hosting service that offers cloud storage and file synchronisation. It is used for file-sharing and collaboration.

http://www.dropbox.com

SharePoint

SharePoint is a browser-based collaboration and document management platform from Microsoft.

https://www.microsoft.com/en-gb/microsoft-365/sharepoint/collaboration

ABOUT THE AUTHOR

Deborah Oxberry has over 25 years' experience of working in health and social care, with 20 of them spent in a business development role. She has worked for both the NHS and large voluntary sector organisations holding positions up to Associate Director level. Debbie was a guest lecturer on the Psychological Therapies course at the University of York.

In July 2014, Deborah set up Mercury Business Development Limited. Mercury worked with a range of organisations to help them win new business, set up business development processes, and train staff to work on bids and tenders. Debbie has now moved on to work as a Business Development Manager in a Social Enterprise specialising in urgent care.

Deborah has an MA and a BA (Hons) in Psychology from the University of Durham, is a Chartered Manager and Fellow of the Chartered Management Institute (CMI), and an Accredited Member of the Association of Proposal Management Professionals (APMP).

Married to Allan since 1991, they live near Durham in the north east of England, with a very curly dog called Ted. In her spare time Deborah studies harp embracing the motto, "you have to practise like the devil to play like an angel!"

HOW TO CONTACT DEBORAH

I would love to hear from you – but only if you promise to be nice!

My website is deborahoxberry.com

You will find me on LinkedIn: https://www.linkedin.com/in/deborahoxberry

DETAILED DISCLAIMERS AND TERMS OF USE

The author of this book and the accompanying materials have used their best efforts in preparing this book. The author makes no representation or warranties with respect to the accuracy applicability, fitness, or completeness of the contents of this book. The information contained in this book is strictly for educational purposes. Therefore, if you wish to apply ideas contained in this book, you are taking full responsibility for your actions.

The author disclaims any warranties (express or implied), merchantability, or fitness for particular purpose. The author shall in no event be held liable to any party for any direct, indirect, punitive, special, incidental or other consequential damages arising directly or indirectly from any use of this material, which is provided "as is", and without warranties. As always the advice of a competent legal, tax, accounting or other professional should be sought.

The author does not warrant the performance, effectiveness or applicability of any sites listed or linked to in this book. All links are for information purposes only and are not warranted for content, accuracy or any other implied or explicit purpose.

Printed in Great Britain
by Amazon